WEST WIND

Other Books by Mary Oliver

POETRY

No Voyage and Other Poems
The River Styx, Ohio, and Other Poems
Twelve Moons
American Primitive
Dream Work
House of Light
New and Selected Poems
White Pine

CHAPBOOKS

The Night Traveler
Sleeping in the Forest

PROSE

A Poetry Handbook
Blue Pastures

MARY OLIVER

West Wind

POEMS AND PROSE POEMS

HOUGHTON MIFFLIN COMPANY *Boston New York 1997*

For information about permission to reproduce selections from
this book, write to Permissions, Houghton Mifflin Company,
215 Park Avenue South, New York, New York 10003.

For information about this and other Houghton Mifflin
trade and reference books and multimedia products, visit The
Bookstore at Houghton Mifflin on the World Wide Web at
http://www.hmco.com/trade/.

Library of Congress Cataloging-in-Publication Data

Oliver, Mary, date.
West wind / Mary Oliver.
p.   cm.
ISBN 0-395-85082-7
I. Title.
PS3565.L5W4   1997
811'.54 — dc21   97-2986   CIP

Design by Anne Chalmers
Typeface: Adobe Garamond

Printed in the United States of America

QUM 10 9 8 7 6 5 4 3 2 1

CONTENTS

Part 1

WEST WIND

Part 1

Some persons of a scientific turn were once discoursing pompously and, to him, distastefully, about the incredible distance of the planets, the length of time light takes to travel to the earth, &c., when he burst out, " 'Tis false! I was walking down a lane the other day, and at the end of it I touched the sky with my stick."

—*Life and Works of William Blake*, A. Gilchrist

Seven White Butterflies

Seven white butterflies
delicate in a hurry look
how they bang the pages
    of their wings as they fly

to the fields of mustard yellow
and orange and plain
gold all eternity
    is in the moment this is what

Blake said Whitman said such
wisdom in the agitated
motions of the mind seven
    dancers floating

even as worms toward
paradise see how they banter
and riot and rise
    to the trees flutter

lob their white bodies into
the invisible wind weightless
lacy willing
    to deliver themselves unto

the universe now each settles
down on a yellow thumb on a
brassy stem now
    all seven are rapidly sipping

from the golden towers who
would have thought it could be so easy?

At Round Pond

owl
make your little appearance now

owl dark bird bird of gloom
messenger reminder

of death
that can't be stopped

argued with leashed put out
like a red fire but

burns as it will
owl

I have not seen you now for
too long a time don't

hide away but come flowing and clacking
the slap of your wings

your death's head oh rise
out of the thick and shaggy pines when you

look down with your
golden eyes how everything

trembles
then settles

from mere incidence into
the lush of meaning.

Black Oaks

Okay, not one can write a symphony, or a dictionary,
    or even a letter to an old friend, full of remembrance
    and comfort.

Not one can manage a single sound, though the blue jays
    carp and whistle all day in the branches, without
    the push of the wind.

But to tell the truth after a while I'm pale with longing
    for their thick bodies ruckled with lichen

and you can't keep me from the woods, from the tonnage
    of their shoulders, and their shining green hair.

Today is a day like any other: twenty-four hours, a
    little sunshine, a little rain.

Listen, says ambition, nervously shifting her weight from
    one boot to another—why don't you get going?

For there I am, in the mossy shadows, under the trees.

And to tell the truth I don't want to let go of the wrists
    of idleness, I don't want to sell my life for money,
    I don't even want to come in out of the rain.

The Dog Has Run Off Again

and I should start shouting his name
and clapping my hands,
but it has been raining all night
and the narrow creek has risen
is a tawny turbulence is rushing along
over the mossy stones
is surging forward
with a sweet loopy music
and therefore I don't want to entangle it
with my own voice
calling summoning
my little dog to hurry back
look the sunlight and the shadows are chasing each other
listen how the wind swirls and leaps and dives up and down
who am I to summon his hard and happy body
his four white feet that love to wheel and pedal
through the dark leaves
to come back to walk by my side, obedient.

Am I Not Among the Early Risers

Am I not among the early risers
and the long-distance walkers?

Have I not stood, amazed, as I consider
the perfection of the morning star
above the peaks of the houses, and the crowns of the trees
    blue in the first light?
Do I not see how the trees tremble, as though
    sheets of water flowed over them
though it is only wind, that common thing,
    free to everyone, and everything?

Have I not thought, for years, what it would be
worthy to do, and then gone off, barefoot and with a silver pail,
    to gather blueberries,
thus coming, as I think, upon a right answer?

What will ambition do for me that the fox, appearing suddenly
at the top of the field,
her eyes sharp and confident as she stared into mine,
has not already done?

What countries, what visitations,
    what pomp
would satisfy me as thoroughly as Blackwater Woods
on a sun-filled morning, or, equally, in the rain?

Here is an amazement—once I was twenty years old and in
    every motion of my body there was a delicious ease,
and in every motion of the green earth there was
    a hint of paradise,
and now I am sixty years old, and it is the same.

Above the modest house and the palace—the same darkness.
Above the evil man and the just, the same stars.

Above the child who will recover and the child who will
      not recover, the same energies roll forward,
from one tragedy to the next and from one foolishness to the next.

      I bow down.

Have I not loved as though the beloved could vanish at any moment,
or become preoccupied, or whisper a name other than mine
      in the stretched curvatures of lust, or over the dinner table?
Have I ever taken good fortune for granted?

Have I not, every spring, befriended the swarm that pours forth?
Have I not summoned the honey-man to come, to hurry,
      to bring with him the white and comfortable hive?

And, while I waited, have I not leaned close, to see everything?
Have I not been stung as I watched their milling and gleaming,
      and stung hard?

Have I not been ready always at the iron door,
      not knowing to what country it opens — to death or to more life?

Have I ever said that the day was too hot or too cold
or the night too long and as black as oil anyway,
or the morning, washed blue and emptied entirely
      of the second-rate, less than happiness

as I stepped down from the porch and set out along
the green paths of the world?

Pilot Snake

had it
lived it would have grown
from twelve inches to a
    hundred maybe would have

set out to eat
all the rats of the world and managed
a few would have frightened
    somebody sooner or later

as it crossed the road would have been
feared and hated and shied away from
black glass lunging
    in the green sea

in the long blades of the grass
but now look death too
is a carpenter how all his
    helpers the shining ants

labor the tiny
knives of their mouths
dipping and slashing how they
    hurry in and out

of that looped body taking
apart opening up now the soul
flashes like a star and is gone there is only
that soft dark building
    death.

So

This morning
    the dogs
        were romping and stomping
            on their nailed feet —

they had hemmed in
    a little thing —
        a field mouse —
            so I picked it up

and held it
    in the purse of my hands,
        where it was safe —
            but it turned

on the blank face
    of my thumb —
        in a burst
            of seedy teeth

it sprinkled
    my whole body with sudden
        nails of pain.
            The dogs

were long gone —
    so under
        an old pine tree,
            on the spicy needles,

I put it down,
    and it dashed away.
        For an instant
            the whole world

was still.
    Then the wind
        fluttered its wrists, a
            sweet music as usual,

though as usual I could not tell
    whether it was about caring or not caring
        that it tossed itself around, in the boughs of light,
        and sang.

Spring

This morning
two birds
fell down the side of the maple tree

like a tuft of fire
a wheel of fire
a love knot

out of control as they plunged through the air
pressed against each other
and I thought

how I meant to live a quiet life
how I meant to live a life of mildness and meditation
tapping the careful words against each other

and I thought—
as though I were suddenly spinning, like a bar of silver
as though I had shaken my arms and *lo!* they were wings—

of the Buddha
when he rose from his green garden
when he rose in his powerful ivory body

when he turned to the long dusty road without end
when he covered his hair with ribbons and the petals of flowers
when he opened his hands to the world.

Stars

Here in my head, language
keeps making its tiny noises.

How can I hope to be friends
with the hard white stars

whose flaring and hissing are not speech
but a pure radiance?

How can I hope to be friends
with the yawning spaces between them

where nothing, ever, is spoken?
Tonight, at the edge of the field,

I stood very still, and looked up,
and tried to be empty of words.

What joy was it, that almost found me?
What amiable peace?

Then it was over, the wind
roused up in the oak trees behind me

and I fell back, easily.
Earth has a hundred thousand pure contraltos —

even the distant night bird
as it talks threat, as it talks love

over the cold, black fields.
Once, deep in the woods,

I found the white skull of a bear
and it was utterly silent —

and once a river otter, in a steel trap,
and it too was utterly silent.

What can we do
but keep on breathing in and out,

modest and willing, and in our places?
Listen, listen, I'm forever saying,

Listen to the river, to the hawk, to the hoof,
to the mockingbird, to the jack-in-the-pulpit—

then I come up with a few words, like a gift.
Even as now.

Even as the darkness has remained the pure, deep darkness.
Even as the stars have twirled a little, while I stood here,

looking up,
one hot sentence after another.

Three Songs

I

A band of wild turkeys is coming down the hill. They are coming slowly — as they walk along they look under the leaves for things to eat, and besides it must be a pleasure to step alternately through the pale sunlight, then patches of slightly golden shade. They are all hens and they lift their thick toes delicately. With such toes they could march up one side of the state and down the other, or skate on water, or dance the tango. But not this morning. As they get closer the sound of their feet in the leaves is like the patter of rain, then rapid rain. My dogs perk their ears, and bound from the path. Instead of opening their dark wings the hens swirl and rush away under the trees, like little ostriches.

2

The meadowlark, with his yellow breast and a sort of limping flight, sings into the morning which, in this case, is perfectly blue, lucid, measureless, and without the least bump of wind. The meadowlark is a spirit, and an epiphany, if I so desire it. I need only to hear him to make something fine, even advisory, of the occasion.

And have you made inquiry yet as to what the poetry of this world is about? For what purpose do we seek it, and ponder it, and give it such value?

And also this is true — that if I consider the golden whistler and the song that pours from his narrow throat in the context of evolution, of reptiles, of Cambrian waters, of the body's wish to change, of the body's incredible crafts and efforts, of life's multitudes, of the winners and the losers, I lose nothing of the original occasion, and its infinite sweetness. For this is my skill — I am capable of pondering the most detailed knowledge, and the most fastened-up, impenetrable mystery, at the same time.

3

There is so much communication and understanding beneath and apart from the substantiations of language spoken out or written down that language is almost no more than a compression, or elaboration—an exactitude, declared emphasis, emotion-in-syntax—not at all essential to the message. And therefore, as an elegance, as something almost superfluous, it is likely (because it is *free* to be so used) to be carefully shaped, to take risks, to begin and even prolong adventures that may turn out poorly after all—and all in the cause of the crisp flight and the buzzing bliss of the words, as well as their directive — to make, of the body-bright commitment to life, and its passions, including (of course!) the passion of meditation, an exact celebration, or inquiry, employing grammar, mirth, and wit in a precise and intelligent way. Language is, in other words, not necessary, but voluntary. If it were necessary, it would have stayed simple; it would not agitate our hearts with ever-present loveliness and ever-cresting ambiguity; it would not dream, on its long white bones, of turning into song.

Shelley

When I'm dying,
    and near paradise,
        maybe
            the little boat will come

like a cloud —
    like a wing —
        like a white light burning.
        This morning,

in the actual fog
    beside the rocking sea,
        there was nothing —
            not a sail,

not a soul.
    There was only this —
        an idea.
            Beauty

can die all right —
    but don't you worry,
        from utter darkness —
            since opposites are, finally, the same —

comes light's snowy field.
    And, as for eternity, what's that
        but the collation of all the hours we have known
        of sweetness

and urgency?
    The boat bounced and sparkled,
        then it trembled,
            then it shook,

then it lay down on the waves.
    I believe in death.
        I believe it is the last wonderful work.
           So they spilled from the boat,

they plunged toward darkness, they drowned.
    You know the story.
        How the sky flares and grows brighter, all the time!
        How time extends!

Maples

The trees have become
suddenly very happy
it is the rain
it is the quick white summer rain

the trees are in motion under it
they are swinging back and forth they are tossing
    the heavy blossoms of their heads
they are twisting their shoulders
even their feet chained to the ground feel good
    thin and gleaming

nobody can prove it but any fool can feel it
they are full of electricity now and the shine isn't just pennies
it pours out from the deepest den
oh pretty trees
    patient   deep-planted

may you have many such days
flinging your bodies in silver circles shaking your heads
over the swamps and the pastures
rimming the fields and the long roads hurrying by.

The Osprey

This morning
an osprey
with its narrow
black-and-white face

and its cupidinous eyes
leaned down
from a leafy tree
to look into the lake — it looked

a long time, then its powerful
shoulders punched out a little
and it fell,
it rippled down

into the water —
then it rose, carrying,
in the clips of its feet,
a slim and limber

silver fish, a scrim
of red rubies
on its flashing sides.
All of this

was wonderful
to look at,
so I simply stood there,
in the blue morning,

looking.
Then I walked away.
Beauty is my work,
but not my only work —

later,
when the fish was gone forever
and the bird was miles away,
I came back

and stood on the shore, thinking—
and if you think
thinking is a mild exercise,
beware!

I mean, I was swimming for my life—
and I was thundering this way and that way
in my shirt of feathers—
and I could not resolve anything long enough

to become one thing
except this: the imaginer.
It was inescapable
as over and over it flung me,

without pause or mercy it flung me
to both sides of the beautiful water—
to both sides
of the knife.

That Sweet Flute John Clare

That sweet flute John Clare;
that broken branch Eddy Whitman;
Christopher Smart, in the press of blazing electricity;
my uncle the suicide;
Woolf on her way to the river;
Wolf, of the sorrowful songs;
Swift, impenetrable murk of Dublin;
Schumann, climbing the bridge, leaping into the Rhine;
Ruskin, Cowper;
Poe, rambling in the gloom-bins of Baltimore and Richmond—

light of the world, hold me.

Sand Dabs, Three

Six black ibis
step through the black and mossy panels
of summer water.

Six times
I sigh with delight.

&

Keep looking.

&

The way a muskrat
in the snick of its teeth can carry
long branches of leaves.

&

Small hawks
cleaning their beaks
in the sun.

&

If you think daylight is just daylight
then it is just daylight.

&

Believe me these are not just words talking.
This is my life, thinking of the darkness to follow.

&

Keep looking.

&

The fox: his barking, in god's darkness, as of a little dog.
The flounce of his teeth.

∽

Every morning
all those pink and green doors
into the sea.

Forty Years

for forty years
the sheets of white paper have
passed under my hands and I have tried
    to improve their peaceful

emptiness putting down
little curls little shafts
of letters words
    little flames leaping

not one page
was less to me than fascinating
discursive full of cadence
    its pale nerves hiding

in the curves of the Qs
behind the soldierly Hs
in the webbed feet of the Ws
    forty years

and again this morning as always
I am stopped as the world comes back
wet and beautiful I am thinking
    that language

is not even a river
is not a tree is not a green field
is not even a black ant traveling
    briskly modestly

from day to day from one
golden page to another.

Black Snake This Time

lay
under the oak trees
in the early morning,
in a half knot,

in a curl,
and, like anyone
catching the runner at rest,
I stared

at that thick black length
whose neck, all summer,
was a river,
whose body was the same river —

whose whole life was a flowing —
whose tail could lash —
who, footless, could spin
like a black tendril and hang

upside down in the branches
gazing at everything
out of seed-shaped red eyes
as it swung to and fro,

the tail making its quick sizzle,
the head lifted
like a black spout.
Was it alive?

Of course it was alive.
This was the quick wrist of early summer,
when everything was alive.
Then I knelt down, I saw

that the snake was gone —
that the face, like a black bud,
had pushed out of the broken petals
of the old year, and it had emerged

on the hundred hoops of its belly,
the tongue sputtering its thread of smoke,
the work of the pearl-colored lung
never pausing, as it pushed

from the chin,
from the crown of the head,
leaving only an empty skin
for the mice to nibble and the breeze to blow

as over the oak leaves and across the creek
and up the far hill it had gone,
damp and shining in the starlight
like a rollicking finger of snow.

Morning Walk

Little by little
the ocean

empties its pockets —
foam and fluff;

and the long, tangled ornateness
of seaweed;

and the whelks,
ribbed or with ivory knobs,

but so knocked about
in the sea's blue hands

that their story is at length only
about the wholeness of destruction —

they come one by one
to the shore

to the shallows
to the mussel-dappled rocks

to the rise to dryness
to the edge of the town

to offer, to the measure that we will accept it,
this wisdom:

though the hour be whole
though the minute be deep and rich

though the heart be a singer of hot red songs
and the mind be as lightning,

what all the music will come to is nothing,
only the sheets of fog and the fog's blue bell —

you do not believe it now, you are not supposed to.
You do not believe it yet—but you will—

morning by singular morning,
and shell by broken shell.

Rain, Tree, Thunder and Lightning

Clouds rolled
from the west—
then they thickened,
then thunder

bucked and boiled
toward the blown woods—
then lightning
slammed down

and opened the tree—
the way a tooth
would open a flower.
I fell down

in the steaming grass,
in the moss,
in the slow things
I was used to

while the branches snapped,
while they shrieked,
while the tree
spat out its solid heart

all over the ground.
Often enough,
even in easy summer,
I think of death—

how it is known to come
by dark, godforsaken inches.
And then I remember
the wheels of the wind,

the heels of the clouds—
the kick of the gold.
What do I hope for
from brother death?

May there be no quibbling.
Like the god that he is
may he slide to the ground
on his golden dial;

and there I will be,
for one last moment,
broken but burning,
like a golden tree.

The Rapture

All summer
    I wandered the fields
        that were thickening
            every morning,

every rainfall,
    with weeds and blossoms,
        with the long loops
            of the shimmering, and the extravagant—

pale as flames they rose
    and fell back,
        replete and beautiful—
            that was all there was—

and I too
    once or twice, at least,
        felt myself rising,
            my boots

touching suddenly the tops of the weeds,
    the blue and silky air—
        listen,
            passion did it,

called me forth,
    addled me,
        stripped me clean
            then covered me with the cloth of happiness—

I think
    there is no other prize,
        only rapture the gleaming,
            rapture the illogical the weightless—

whether it be for the perfect shapeliness
    of something you love—
        like an old German song—
        or of someone—

or the dark floss of the earth itself,
    heavy and electric.
        At the edge of sweet sanity open
        such wild, blind wings.

Fox

You don't ever know where
a sentence will take you, depending
on its roll and fold. I was walking
over the dunes when I saw
the red fox asleep under the green
branches of the pine. It flared up
in the sweet order of its being,
the tail that was over the muzzle
lifting in airy amazement
and the fire of the eyes followed
and the pricked ears and the thin
barrel body and the four
athletic legs in their black stockings and it
came to me how the polish of the world changes
everything, I was hot I was cold I was almost
dead of delight. Of course the mind keeps
cool in its hidden palace — yes, the mind takes
a long time, is otherwise occupied than by
happiness, and deep breathing. Still,
at last, it comes too, running
like a wild thing, to be taken
with its twin sister, breath. So I stood
on the pale, peach-colored sand, watching the fox
as it opened like a flower, and I began
softly, to pick among the vast assortment of words
that it should run again and again across the page
that you again and again should shiver with praise.

Gratitude

I was walking the field,
in the fatness of spring
the field was flooded with water, water stained black,
black from the tissues of leaves, oak mostly, but also
beech, also
blueberry, bay.

Then the big hawk rose. In her eyes
I could see how thoroughly she
hated me. And there was her nest, like a round raft

with three white eggs in it, just

above the black water.

                                    ℮⌁

She floats away	Halfway to my knees
climbs the invisible air	in the black water
on her masculine wings	I look up
then glides back	I cannot stop looking up
agitated responsible	how much time has passed
climbs again angry	I can hardly see her now
does not look at me.	swinging in that blue blaze.

                                    ℮⌁

There are days when I rise from my desk desolate.
There are days when the field water and the slender grasses
    and the wild hawks
have it all over the rest of us

whether or not they make clear sense, ride the beautiful
long spine of grammar, whether or not they rhyme.

Little Summer Poem Touching the Subject of Faith

Every summer
    I listen and look
        under the sun's brass and even
            in the moonlight, but I can't hear

anything, I can't see anything—
    not the pale roots digging down, nor the green stalks muscling up,
        nor the leaves
            deepening their damp pleats,

nor the tassels making,
    nor the shucks, nor the cobs.
        And still,
            every day,

the leafy fields
    grow taller and thicker—
        green gowns lofting up in the night,
            showered with silk.

And so, every summer,
    I fail as a witness, seeing nothing—
        I am deaf too
            to the tick of the leaves,

the tapping of downwardness from the banyan feet—
    all of it
        happening
            beyond all seeable proof, or hearable hum.

And, therefore, let the immeasurable come.
    Let the unknowable touch the buckle of my spine.
        Let the wind turn in the trees,
            and the mystery hidden in dirt

swing through the air.
    How could I look at anything in this world
        and tremble, and grip my hands over my heart?
        What should I fear?

One morning
    in the leafy green ocean
        the honeycomb of the corn's beautiful body
        is sure to be there.

Dogs

Over
the wide field

the dark deer
went running,

five dogs
screaming

at his flanks,
at his heels,

my own two darlings
among them

lunging and buckling
with desire

as they leaped
for the throat

as they tried
and tried again

to bring him down.
At the lake

the deer
plunged —

I could hear
the green wind

of his breath
tearing

but the long legs
never stopped

till he clambered
up the far shore.

The dogs
moaned and screeched

they flung themselves
on the grass

panting
and steaming.

It took hours
but finally

in the half-drowned light
in the silence

of the summer evening
they woke

from fitful naps,
they stepped

in their old good natures
toward us

look look
into their eyes

bright as planets
under the long lashes

here is such happiness when you speak their names!
here is such unforced love!

here is such shyness such courage!
here is the shining rudimentary soul

here is hope retching, the world as it is
here is the black the red the bottomless pool.

At the Shore

This morning
   wind that light-limbed dancer was all
      over the sky while
         ocean slapped up against
            the shore's black-beaked rocks
row after row of waves
   humped and fringed and exactly
different from each other and
   above them one white gull
      whirled slant and fast then
         dipped its wings turned
            in a soft and descending decision its
leafy feet touched
   pale water just beyond
breakage of waves it settled
   shook itself opened
      its spoony beak cranked
         like a pump. Listen!
            Here is the white and silky trumpet of nothing.
Here is the beautiful Nothing, body of happy,
   meaningless fire, wildfire, shaking the heart.

At Great Pond

At Great Pond
the sun, rising,
scrapes his orange breast
on the thick pines,

and down tumble
a few orange feathers into
the dark water.
On the far shore

a white bird is standing
like a white candle—
or a man, in the distance,
in the clasp of some meditation—

while all around me the lilies
are breaking open again
from the black cave
of the night.

Later, I will consider
what I have seen—
what it could signify—
what words of adoration I might

make of it, and to do this
I will go indoors to my desk—
I will sit in my chair—
I will look back

into the lost morning
in which I am moving, now,
like a swimmer,
so smoothly,

so peacefully,
I am almost the lily—
almost the bird vanishing over the water
on its sleeves of light.

Part 2

WEST WIND

WEST WIND

If there is life after the earth-life, will you come with me?
Even then? Since we're bound to be something, why not
together. Imagine! Two little stones, two fleas under the
wing of a gull, flying along through the fog! Or, ten blades
of grass. Ten loops of honeysuckle, all flung against each
other, at the edge of Race Road! Beach plums! Snowflakes,
coasting into the winter woods, making a very small sound,
like this

    sooooooooooooooooooooooooooooooooooooooooooooooo

as they marry the dusty bodies of the pitch-pines. Or, rain —
that gray light running over the sea, pocking it, lacquering
it, coming, all morning and afternoon, from the west wind's
youth and abundance and jollity — pinging and jangling
down upon the roofs of Provincetown.

2

You are young. So you know everything. You leap
into the boat and begin rowing. But, listen to me.
Without fanfare, without embarrassment, without
any doubt, I talk directly to your soul. Listen to me.
Lift the oars from the water, let your arms rest, and
your heart, and heart's little intelligence, and listen to
me. There is life without love. It is not worth a bent
penny, or a scuffed shoe. It is not worth the body of a
dead dog nine days unburied. When you hear, a mile
away and still out of sight, the churn of the water
as it begins to swirl and roil, fretting around the
sharp rocks—when you hear that unmistakable
pounding—when you feel the mist on your mouth
and sense ahead the embattlement, the long falls
plunging and steaming—then row, row for your life
toward it.

3

And the speck of my heart, in my shed of flesh and bone, began to sing out, the way the sun would sing if the sun could sing, if light had a mouth and a tongue, if the sky had a throat, if god wasn't just an idea but shoulders and a spine, gathered from everywhere, even the most distant planets, blazing up. Where am I? Even the rough words come to me now, quick as thistles. Who made your tyrant's body, your thirst, your delving, your gladness? Oh tiger, oh bone-breaker, oh tree on fire! Get away from me. Come closer.

4

But how did you come burning down like a
wild needle, knowing
just where my heart was?

5

There are night birds, in the garden below us, singing.
Oh, listen!
For a moment I thought it was
our own bodies.

6

When the sun goes down
the roses
fling off their red dresses
and put on their black dresses

the wind is coming
over the sandy streets
of the town called moonlight

with his long arms
with his silver mouth
his hands

humorous at first
then serious
then crazy

touching their faces their dark petals
until they begin rising and falling:
the honeyed seizures.

All day they have been busy being roses
gazing responsible over the sand
into the sky into the blue ocean

so now why not
a little comfort
a little rippling pleasure.

ↄ

You there, puddled in lamplight at your midnight desk—
you there, rewriting nature
so anyone can understand it—

what will you say about the roses —
their sighing, their tossing —
and the want of the heart,

and the trill of the heart,
and the burning mouth
of the wind?

7

We see Bill only occasionally, when we stop by the antique shop that's on the main hot highway to Charlottesville. Usually he's alone — his wife is dead — but sometimes his son will be with him, or idling just outside in the yard. Once M. bought a small glass ship from the boy, it had chips of colored glass for sails and cost two dollars, the boy was greatly pleased.

Today Bill tells us — for a mockingbird has begun to sing — how a friend came during the summer and filled a bowl with fruit from the cherry tree. Then, leaving the bowl on the stoop, he went inside to sit with Bill at the kitchen table. Together Bill and his friend watched the mockingbird come to the bowl, take the cherries one by one, fly back across the yard and drop them under the branches of the tree. When the bowl was empty the bird settled again in the leaves and began to sing vigorously.

At the back of the shop and here and there on the dusty shelves are piled the useless broken things one couldn't ever sell — bits of rusty metal, and odd pieces of china, a cup or a plate with a fraction of its design still clear: a garden, or a span of country bridge leading from one happiness or another, or part of a house. Once Bill told us, almost shyly, how much the boy is coming to resemble his mother. Through the open window we can hear the mockingbird, still young, still lucky, wild beak kissing and chuckling as it flutters and struts along the avenue of song.

8

The young, tall English poet—soon to die, soon to sail on his small boat into the blue haze and then the storm and then under the gray waves' spinning threshold—went over to Pisa to meet a friend; met him; spent with him a sunny afternoon. I love this poet, which means nothing here or there, but is like a garden in my heart. So my love is a gift to myself. And I think of him, on that July afternoon in Pisa, while his friend Hunt told him stories pithy and humorous, of their friends in England, so that he began to laugh, so that his tall, lean body shook, and his long legs couldn't hold him, and he had to lean up against the building, seized with laughter, abundant and unstoppable; and so he leaned in the wild sun, against the stones of the building, with the tears flying from his eyes—full of foolishness, howling, hanging on to the stones, crawling with laughter, clasping his own body as it began to fly apart in the nonsense, the sweetness, the intelligence, the bright happiness falling, like tiny gold flowers, like the sunlight itself, the lilt of Hunt's voice, on this simple afternoon, with a friend, in Pisa.

9

And what did you think love would be like? A summer day? The brambles in their places, and the long stretches of mud? Flowers in every field, in every garden, with their soft beaks and their pastel shoulders? On one street after another, the litter ticks in the gutter. In one room after another, the lovers meet, quarrel, sicken, break apart, cry out. One or two leap from windows. Most simply lean, exhausted, their thin arms on the sill. They have done all that they could. The golden eagle, that lives not far from here, has perhaps a thousand tiny feathers flowing from the back of its head, each one shaped like an infinitely small but perfect spear.

10

Dark is as dark does.

❧

Something with the smallest wings shakes itself
from under a thumb of bark.

The ocean breathes in its silver jacket.

❧

Outside, hanging on the trellis, in the moonlight,
     the flowers are opening, each one
as fancy in its unfurl as a difficult thought.

❧

So we cross the dark together.

❧

Outside: the almost liquid beauty of the flowers.

❧

Now the linnets wake.
Now the pearls of their voices are falling
     in the morning light.

❧

Did we sleep long? Is it this life still, or
is it the next life, already? Are we gone, then?
Are we there?

❧

How will we ever know?

II

Now only the humorous shadows that the moon makes, playing the corners of furniture, flung and dropped clothing, the backs of books, the architecture of electronics, and so on. The bed that level and soft rise is empty. We are gone.

So, say that dreams, possibilities, emotions, while we are gone from the house, take shape. Say there are thirty at least, one to represent each year, and more leaning in the doorway between the slope of the beach and the pale walls of the rooms, just moon-gazing for a moment or two, before they come into that starry garden, our house at night.

Some of those thirty are as awkward as children, romping and gripping. Others have become birds, clouds, trees dipping their heart-shaped leaves, that long song. Here and there a face that won't trans-form—eyes of stone, expressions of pettiness and sulk. And now it is winter, and in the black air the snow is falling in its own sweet leisure, for its own reasons. And now the snow has deepened, and created form: two white ponies. How they gallop in the waves. How they steam, and turn to look for each other. How they love the clouds and the tender, long grass and the horizons and the hills. How they nuzzle, how they nicker, how they reach down, at the unclosable spring in the notch of the pasture, to be replenished.

12

The cricket did not actually seek the hearth, but the thicket of carpet beneath the refrigerator. The whirring above was company, and from it issued night and day the most prized gift of the gods: warmth. Especially in the evenings the cricket was happy, and sang. Later, in the night, it crept out. There was not a single night when it did not find, sooner or later, a sweet crumb, and a small plump seed of some sort between the floorboards. Thus, it got used to hope. It revised altogether its idea of what the world was like, and of what was going to happen next, or, even, eventually. It thought: how sufficient are these empty rooms! It thought: here I am still, in my black suit, warm and content—and drew a little music from its dark thighs. As though the twilight underneath the refrigerator were the world. As though the winter would never come.

13

It is midnight, or almost.
Out in the world the wind stretches
bundles back into itself like a hundred
bolts of lace then stretches again

flows itself over the windowsill and into the room

it scatters the papers from the desk
    it is in love with disorganization

now the manuscript is on the floor, and reshuffled
now the chapters have married each other
now the alphabet is lost
now the white curtains are tossing wing on wing
now the body of the wind snaps

it sniffs the closet it touches into the pockets of the coats
it touches the shells upon the shelves
it touches the tops of the books
it slides along the walls

now the lamplight wavers
as the body of the wind swings over the light
outside a million stars are burning
now the ocean calls to the wind

now the wind like water slips under the sash
into the yard the garden the long black sky

in my room after such disturbance I sit, smiling.
I pick up a pencil, I put it down, I pick it up again.
I am thinking of you.
I am always thinking of you.

Part 3

Have You Ever Tried to Enter the Long Black Branches

Have you ever tried to enter the long black branches
    of other lives—
tried to imagine what the crisp fringes, full of honey,
    hanging
from the branches of the young locust trees, in early summer,
    feel like?

Do you think this world is only an entertainment for you?

Never to enter the sea and notice how the water divides
    with perfect courtesy, to let you in!
Never to lie down on the grass, as though you were the grass!
Never to leap to the air as you open your wings over
    the dark acorn of your heart!

No wonder we hear, in your mournful voice, the complaint
    that something is missing from your life!

Who can open the door who does not reach for the latch?
Who can travel the miles who does not put one foot
    in front of the other, all attentive to what presents itself
    continually?
Who will behold the inner chamber who has not observed
    with admiration, even with rapture, the outer stone?

Well, there is time left—
fields everywhere invite you into them.

And who will care, who will chide you if you wander away
    from wherever you are, to look for your soul?

Quickly, then, get up, put on your coat, leave your desk!

To put one's foot into the door of the grass, which is
   the mystery, which is death as well as life, and
   not be afraid!

To set one's foot in the door of death, and be overcome
   with amazement!

To sit down in front of the weeds, and imagine
   god the ten-fingered, sailing out of his house of straw,

nodding this way and that way, to the flowers of the
   present hour,

to the song falling out of the mockingbird's pink mouth,

to the tiplets of the honeysuckle, that have opened
   in the night.

To sit down, like a weed among weeds, and rustle in the wind!

ᴇᴙ

Listen, are you breathing just a little, and calling it a life?

While the soul, after all, is only a window,
and the opening of the window no more difficult
than the wakening from a little sleep.

ᴇᴙ

Only last week I went out among the thorns and said
   to the wild roses:
deny me not,
but suffer my devotion.
Then, all afternoon, I sat among them. Maybe

I even heard a curl or two of music, damp and rouge-red,
hurrying from their stubby buds, from their delicate watery bodies.

ᴇᴙ

For how long will you continue to listen to those dark shouters,
    caution and prudence?

Fall in! Fall in!

⌀

A woman standing in the weeds.
A small boat flounders in the deep waves, and what's coming next
    is coming with its own heave and grace.

⌀

Meanwhile, once in a while, I have chanced, among the quick things,
    upon the immutable.
What more could one ask?

And I would touch the faces of the daisies,
and I would bow down
to think about it.

That was then, which hasn't ended yet.

Now the sun begins to swing down. Under the peach-light,
I cross the fields and the dunes, I follow the ocean's edge.

I climb. I backtrack.
I float.
I ramble my way home.

ACKNOWLEDGMENTS

My thanks to the editors of the following magazines in which some of these poems, sometimes in slightly different form, have previously been printed.

Amicus, The cricket...; At the Shore; Sand Dabs, Three

Appalachia, Black Oaks, The Dog Has Run Off Again

Country Journal, The Osprey

Michigan Quarterly Review, At Round Pond

Ohio Review, And what did you think love would be like?

Orion, The Rapture

Poetry, Forty Years, Pilot Snake

Provincetown Arts, Dogs, Shelley, Stars, You are young...,
    If there is life after the earth-life...

Shenandoah, Three Songs, Seven White Butterflies

The Southern Review, Spring